# A Ray of Sunshine

# A Ray of Sunshine

## The Perfect Storm

**Lynette Shelto-Johnson**

Copyright 2024 The Lynette Shelto-Johnson book,
London, England 2024
First published 2024
English translation 2024

Lynette Shelto-Johnson has asserted her right under the copyright design to be identified as the author of this book. This book is entirely a work of non-fiction.

This book is sold subject to the condition that it shall not by way of trade or otherwise be lent, resold, hired out or otherwise circulated other than that which it is published and without similar condition, including this condition being imposed on the subsequent purchaser.

This book contains portions of quoted Bible text from the King James Version.

ISBNs
Paperback: 978-1-80541-546-6
eBook: 978-1-80541-547-3

# Contents

Introduction ................................................................ 1

Storm Clouds ............................................................. 7

Falsely Accused ......................................................... 15

Brokenness ............................................................... 21

Forgiveness ............................................................... 35

Faith and Hope ......................................................... 45

Failures ..................................................................... 53

Personal Revival ........................................................ 63

Success ..................................................................... 75

Giving Thanks .......................................................... 87

Reasons for Writing This Book ................................. 93

Book Summary ........................................................ 97

Acknowledgements ................................................. 101

# Introduction

The contents of this book, *A Ray of Sunshine,* focus on failures, brokenness, personal revival and success in depth. I believe that giving up should never be an option at any time.

The dawn shall come for the beginning of a phenomenon time. It could be a favourable one.

Failures are stepping stones to victory. Anytime there is a failure, think about all your past successes. This will help you to reduce the amount of emotional impact your life will have from your failure. This is not a terrible thing. It is only a disappointment and a delay on the road to success.

We all have had a physical fall or two at some point in our lives. Did we stay down where we fell? The answer is no. We often rise from where we fall. It is the same as when we have failures. We take the failure as a lesson learnt and we can look back and reflect on our mistakes. This is why we have the reflection tool. Once you know what the mistakes were, the lesson will equip you with the necessary knowledge to attain success in the future. Failures are stepping stones to improve your life, to take you on to succeed. You should never let failure stop you from your set goal.

Most great men and women achieved success after failures. Their accomplishments were achieved after discouraging hours. They made it to the top because they fought against those discouraging hours. They fought against failures. They did not give up. They fought against the struggle, and they never gave up. This is something that is difficult, but with motivation, persistence, resilience, hard work and prayer, the result is success. I know how difficult that is because I have been there and done that. I am happy that I never gave up on my dreams. That is another reason why I encourage everyone not to give up on their dreams.

Love is powerful. Love is kind. Love is generous. Love is the answer to all of life's situations because God himself is love. Hope begins when you stand in the dark, looking out to the light.

Sometimes a rainbow can be seen after the storm. Trouble and trials will come, but remember these do not last always. A miracle happens every single day of your life. You are given the opportunity to live another day and to experience what the world has to offer, and that is something you must always remember and appreciate. Be grateful and be thankful for life.

This book will give you emotional support when life is not going as you would like it to go.

Introduction

It is in our darkest hours that we may discover the true strength of God's light within us. God has given us a light to carry, so others can understand something clearly: God is within us. So, let us continue to shine that light so billions can move from darkness and into God's marvellous light.

In trouble, we either stay and struggle or we fight with the strength of God's light within us to overcome our troubles. For we wrestle not against flesh and blood, but against principalities, against powers, against the rulers of the darkness of this world, against spiritual wickedness in high places. That is why we pray and put God first in everything, so he can save us in the time of trouble.

I do believe that there are people out there who need our help in so many ways. I choose to help by sharing inspiring, motivating and uplifting messages on social media. I also thought there might be people who love reading books to pass away the free time. I thought, *Why not write inspirational messages in the form of a book?* This book will benefit anyone who reads it in so many ways.

Before I go any further, let me introduce myself. My name is Lynette Shelto-Johnson and I live in London. I was born in the beautiful country of Guyana which is in South America close to the Caribbean.

I am a nurse by profession and part-time writer. I am a mother of one daughter. Her name is Crystal. I gave her that name because it means pure and clear. To God be praised and glorified.

Thank God for his grace and mercies that are new each morning. The word of God is profound and inspiring, and his words motivate us to live a life for him. You and I are beacons for bringing God's creations from darkness into his marvellous light in this dying world. We should have faith in God, which is like unseen steps to victory.

Just looking around the world, we can see that Bible prophecies are being fulfilled. Nations are fighting against nations. Wars and rumours of wars. People are fighting for power. Rulers are fighting for land of another country. Only God can save us in these perilous times. There is no hiding place on Earth. Let us stay on the side of the good Lord and share the love of God.

Remember, you and I are all heroes in our own little stories. We do not have to be rich or a celebrity to be a shining star for God. Let us use the light we carry, so others can see the path of God.

I have learnt not to let my past define who I am or define my future. Do not get stranded in any one of your conditions or circumstances. Focus on your dream and realise that beyond your situation lies greater heights. You can attain greater success that will take you to your victories, greater strength and greater anointing from God. Be grateful in everything that happens. Always remember

## Introduction

everything happens for a reason and a season. Everything leaves you a lesson.

I pray that God grants us all a peaceful and blessed life. I pray that God continues to bless us all, our families, friends and others out there. May his light and favours continue to shine on us and grant us peace and joy. Amen.

# Storm Clouds

The first thing that should come to mind is, despite whatever happens, the sun always shines after the storm. Storm clouds do not always last in the physical sense. Storm clouds always pass over.

Despite the unprecedented times, God's grace and mercies are glorious memories of the past and his grace and mercies are still given freely to us today. God's love is powerful. God's love is kind. His love is generous. God's love is the answer to all of life's situations because God himself is love.

Before telling lies about another person to destroy their life, take a step back and think before telling that lie. Think about the different consequences of the danger and damage you could cause for those who you fabricate things about due to any evil intentions. This could cause someone's life to be turned upside down. Avoid causing problems for others by not saying things you have no idea are true or not. You don't know what would happen to that person. Avoid stormy days for people by always speaking the truth.

People are saying wrong is right and right is wrong. There are also people who are saying there is no God. There are people who do not believe in eternal life. Also, there are people who do not believe that Jesus rose from the dead. We are living in serious times. We are living in tribulation times. The shaking and shifting times are on us. Unprecedented and uncertain times are on us. Where shall we stand in these times without the good Lord on our side? Billions are still going down the broad road to destruction. Only a small percentage of people are walking the narrow road to life eternal.

The harvesting time Is still on and the workers for God's harvesting of souls is getting less and less. I pray that God will touch and anoint us to tidy up our lives for him, so we can help save souls for the kingdom of God. The probation door will soon be closed, and people will be left out of the kingdom of God if we do not put away from all selfish ways and pride before the coming of the Lord.

I pray that God grants anointing and healing to all those who are sick and aching from one thing or another. There are people who feel like their life is like a storm. These people need reassurance that things can get better for them once they believe in themselves and believe that God will help them. An umbrella does not stop the rain, but it allows us to stand in the rain or walk in the rain without getting wet. Just like faith in God, do not remove our trials and troubles, as faith gives us the strength to overcome them.

God did not give us a spirit of fear, but he gave us a spirit of courage. He promised to be there with us always in good and troubled times. His peace, love and joy will comfort and strengthen our hearts. Let us always remember this and carry this thought in our minds.

On a stormy day, the place looks dark and there is no sight of the sun. There is always a prayer and wish in the minds of people that the storm will soon be over. There is always hope for the sunshine to come through the clouds.

During the storms, people feel anxious and fear the unknown. This is because most storms cause damage to people's lives, properties and other things. There are places where the damage may be more than other places. It is the same as a great tidal wave. When it comes to the land, it takes everything in its way back out. The storms of life may be physical storms or emotional storms. With both types of storms, we need to be mentally strong to cope with the aftermath of them.

Sometimes there are people who are living in places which are prone to storms and hurricanes. These people set their minds to prepare for the storms and what comes with them.

People might say to you that they are not afraid of storms because their lives are already like a storm. Things will never be perfect, until Jesus comes again.

In any of life's situations, there will sometimes be storms. But God still performs miracles in every situation. In every storm, God shines his light.

Unconditional love stands the test of time. Only in God are we be able to share true love within this world. Love is the greatest gift because God himself is love. The good Lord is all powerful and he saves us in any stormy situation of our lives. Thank the Lord for his supernatural power. Let us remember life goes quickly, but kindness and love last forever, because God is love.

Sometimes the hardest roads lead to the best destinations.

*And the Lord, he it is that doth go before thee; he will be with thee, he will not fail thee, neither forsake thee: fear not, neither be dismayed. (Deuteronomy 31:8)*

We need to dance in the rain until the storm is over. Sometimes we need to pray that there is no storm and focus on the positive things during the unprecedented times. Praying is a powerful act that helps us to communicate with God. Prayer changes situations.

Evil strives when good men and women stand back and do nothing.

The Bible tells us: "Let your light so shine before men, that they may see your good works, and glorify your Father which is in heaven." (Matthew 5:16)

## Storm Clouds

When everything is going against you, remember that the aeroplane takes off against the wind, not with it. Hardships often prepare ordinary people for an extraordinary destiny.

Our difficulties may feel heavy, but their weight is designed to drive us closer to God, strengthening us and anchoring us to the steady hope of his love.

Circumstances and problems may keep coming. Do not let them control your life. Focus on your best action plans to limit these to an extent that you can still live a good and happy life.

People's problems can be revealed on their faces. Learn to smile within your problems. Practise dancing in the rain until the storm is over. Sometimes people like me use this mechanism to mask their problems. Grumbling about your problems can make you feel worse. Instead, pray and ask God to direct your path to a speedy solution to the problem. Speaking to the right people about your problem may help you to reduce the emotional burden of the problem. You may be able to get ideas of how to solve the problem.

Another way of reducing the stress of your problem is by helping another person who needs help. This will bring joy to your heart until you figure out how to solve your own problem. Helping others who are going through a comparable situation to yours is a positive and inspiring thing to do.

The perfect storm is when God allows us to go through the challenging times that will land us right into victory. Sometimes God allows us to go through the storm to build our faith then he brings us the calm for a brighter day.

It may sound easy to tell someone to try to think positively always, especially if that person is in a dangerous situation or a challenging situation.

When life looks dark, and in every aspect of your life there seems to be no solution, do not give up on God. He will help you to find a way out in the wilderness. If God does not change our situation, he will give us the faith to walk through the storm. A positive mental attitude is one of the keys to surviving the challenges of life. There are certain things beyond our control, but we can control our attitude. The attitude we decide to keep will determine whether we overcome our challenges or whether they overcome us.

There are people who want happiness, but no one wants pain. We cannot have a rainbow without a little rain. Just enjoy the little things in life because one day you will look back and realise they were indeed the massive things. Learn to enjoy life and dance through the rain until the storm is over.

It does not matter what your situation is. Remember, God is still in control, and he is still on his throne. He is the creator of the universe, and he determines everything.

Keep praying to him. Keep trusting him. Keep hope and faith alive. Trust God even where you do not understand. As the lighthouse guides the ships to safety in storms, God will guide us to safety in life's storms.

# Falsely Accused

This can make someone mentally unwell. It is just like an emotional storm. People who share false allegations about other people do not have love in their hearts. These are people who have bad intentions towards others. I know of family and friends who have been in such a dreadful situation, and it can be destructive to people's lives.

I have learnt that people who spread false allegations about others will have karma reach them. I believe in God's judgement on those people. The Bible tells us: "For whatsoever a man soweth, that shall he also reap." (Galatians 6:7)

Having the mind to accuse others wrongfully is saying something about such types of people. These types of people are mentally disturbed, and they need urgent help to revive themselves from such a destructive mind.

Evil can never overcome good. This means it only appears as if evil is winning. Good will always triumph over evil. Just like light will always overcome darkness. Those people who have evil destructive minds and harm others need urgent emotional help. They need physiological counselling as their sick minds permit them to commit evil intentions to innocent people. These are unhappy people. These are people who do not know what love is. These are people who feel that their lives are not worth anything, so they need to destroy other people's lives as well. People with evil intentions live their lives finding ways to destroy other people's lives. Accusing others wrongfully of things they know nothing of can be damaging to a person's emotional status, their character and so much more. Even when the truth is out, the emotional strain of the falsely accused will still be a disturbing memory to remember.

For people who like to gossip, think about what you are spreading verbally. Make sure the news you are spreading is true and not news that will be destructive to others. Sometimes people spread untrue gossip, so do not get caught up in such a wasteful hobby. Be someone who can help stop gossip, especially false allegations.

We all have been there some time or another when someone may have said something about us that is a hundred percent fiction. This can be a painful process to go through. Even if you try to protect your name, there will always be someone else who might believe the person who spread the false news. People with bad intentions will make the false allegations sound factual.

I have been there where I heard things that I had never even heard or knew about. I am sure there are people who have experienced the same situation of being falsely accused, so you can relate to what I am talking about. Haters love spreading inaccurate information.

One of my nephews went through a similar situation where he was falsely accused of something he knew nothing about. He spoke the truth, but the truth was denied, and the false allegations were believed instead. God does not sleep, so God allowed videos to appear which revealed the truth.

The evil one will always try to put a good person down, but God promised to guide and protect his people. The joy of the Lord will continue to be the strength of his people. The evil one will try to strip others of everything they worked hard for and everything they have, but God shall bless that person back twofold after the evil one causes destruction.

For those of you who have gone through similar situations, please keep praying and keep trusting God for deliverance. Judgement Day shall come for all those people who love to spread false allegations about people for evil intentions.

God is good and his grace and mercies are new each morning. Hang in there and trust God for a renewal of your emotional status.

When you are falsely accused, I know it is a painful thing because I have been there, and God delivered me with the truth. The only way we can overcome the pain of being falsely accused is by forgiving those who falsely accused us. If you do not forgive the offenders, you will not be able to free yourself from the aches and pains from the dreadful occurrence.

Remember, to err is human and to forgive is divine. Forgive and let that inner peace and joy flow within your heart and mind. Free up your mind. Do not let any person with bad intentions steal your joy because the joy of the Lord is our strength and shield.

You need to free your mind, release and let go of the pain from all the terrible things people have done to you. When you do that, your mind will be free to move on with your life. Do not forget to pray for your enemies.

Continue to walk with your head high and shoulders square. Be proud of yourself and always put God first. Remember to be thankful for what you have and do not worry about what you do not have. God will take care of your future necessities. May God continue to bless you and your family during these unprecedented and uncertain times. Let the light you carry continue to shine within and outwards.

Victory and deliverance belong to God. We give not to receive, but we give knowing God will bless us in return. We are kind to people, even though people may not be kind to us in return. This is the beautiful world we are living in where sometimes it may seem unfair that people may not treat us as good as we treat them. Please do not let your heart be troubled. Jesus was sinless, yet they crucified him. Judas was one of Jesus' own, yet he betrayed Jesus. Who are we that people would not do unjust things to us? None of us is perfect.

Let us continue to love one another. Not everyone may like us, but this is a world of sin, so we cannot expect better. Jonah was not perfect, but God chose him to take the warning message to Nineveh for the evil people to change their lives and accept God. Jonah was disobedient and that is why the whale swallowed him. Thankfully, miraculously, he still ended up on Nineveh's shore. Thankfully, the people of Nineveh turned from their wicked ways and accepted the Lord. Jonah's mission was completed, yet he wanted God to destroy Nineveh even though the people changed their lives. What a selfish man Jonah was to wish for the people to die, but God is a merciful God, and he spared the lives of those people. Victory and deliverance belong to God.

Faith, obedience and good work are vital for a good and happy life. God will make wonderful things happen in your life, regardless of what you are experiencing now. It may take a while, but God is always on time for miracles. Continue to do good. Shine your light in the world. Then people will see the good work and they will glorify God.

## A Ray of Sunshine

It may seem difficult, but God can make things possible. God will move for you. Stay in faith even when others doubt you and mistreat you. Know that God is working. Keep trusting and believing, and he will vindicate you at the right time.

# Brokenness

The sun is a daily reminder that we too can rise again from the darkness, that we too can shine our own light. Brokenness is like falling. We do not want anyone to see us when we fall, so we usually rise quickly. When you are in any demanding situation, most of the time we do not want anyone to know, so we keep it to ourselves. There are falls where we may sometimes need others to help us get up. It is the same as when we are in any inconvenient situation and we may need others to help us out of those situations. It is important that you choose carefully who you would like to help you out of any demanding situation. Sometimes we can do things alone and sometimes we need the help of others.

When we are feeling unhappy about something, we may not want to talk about it at first. There may be people who are particularly good at covering up bad situations. You may ask them how they are, and they will say they are doing fine. In most cases, we believe them because they may say it with a smile. Smiles can sometimes be deceiving. There are people who will smile with you when their life is upside down. Most of the time, these are people who have the joy of the Lord in their hearts, so demanding situations do not make them unhappy.

There are people who sometimes seem grumpy and always have a cold stare. We may sometimes assume that these are not nice people. It is good to try to hold friendly conversations with these types of people. Most of the time, when we assume that someone is unfriendly, it is because these types of people are sad. Mental health is a difficult topic to deal with, but it is something that everyone should look out for when we suggest a person is having difficulties. Brokenness can be a devastating thing for someone if they do not have help on time. People need to get help as quickly as possible when dealing with emotional trauma. If not, it will be more difficult for their healing process.

When I was a child, I used to say to myself that when I fell in love, it had to be forever. I have always loved my family and friends. I went to church and always tried my best to do the will of God, but that was not enough. I always thought I was close enough to God, but never knew I still needed to get closer. I tried harder and harder, but it was not enough, because we are not close to God until we get a personal spiritual encounter with him.

Sometimes the Devil tries hard to steal our joy, but God's peace and joy conquer all. The past thirteen years were a trying and testing time for me and my family. I lost my mum, my dad, three aunts and a nephew. But glory be to God. His peace and love cover my fears, pain and sadness. But within those thirteen years, Satan thought I would have lost faith in God, but miraculously, that was the time I developed a close encounter with God. God granted me faith, joy and peace within my brokenness. The storms of life will always be easier once God is on our side.

During those trying times, strangely, I found the true love of God. During those trying times, I found true love when I had a close spiritual encounter with the Lord. I am grateful to God for protecting me and my family physically and emotionally throughout those raging storms of life.

This is why I have shared love every day since then. All the previous years, I was doing God's will, but I still did not know the Lord on a personal level, but I do now.

Christmas time sometimes makes me sad as my father and one of my aunts died during Christmas time, but I still celebrate Christmas because the peace and love of Jesus gives me strength. I remember it like it was yesterday when my father was sick during Christmas of 2009. It was a sad Christmas as my mind was thinking about my father's sickness. Sadly, my father passed away on 28 December 2009, which makes it difficult to celebrate the new year. Instead of celebrating that year, my family and I were organising my father's funeral. May his soul continue to rest in peace. How can one enjoy Christmas and celebrate after losing one's father? It was a grim time, but the good Lord gave us peace, comfort and joy.

The Christmas season is a time when love rises higher in the air. It was that same time over two thousand years ago, when our saviour entered the world through the eastern skies. It was the time when the peace dove flew over the raging battlefield, and all guns went down miraculously. God had brought peace to the western front.

For all those who are feeling down today, rise and shine with the peace, faith, love and joy of the Lord, and let it be your strength. Let us do what we do best: smile within our storms. For it is better to be a blessing to another person than to receive a blessing. Blessings are all around us. You and I are all blessings from the almighty God. We are children of God's royal priesthood.

Just remember, people do not cure themselves, God does. There is no such thing as wasted prayers. So, hang in there. Your dawn is coming in Jesus' name. Amen.

We should love all and God loves us too with an unconditional and everlasting love.

Someone could be depressed without showing any symptoms. Be kind. Here is something I have learnt firsthand. No matter how someone looks or act, you truly never know what is happening in their lives. There will be people who smile when you greet them and carry a pleasant conversation. In short, they put on a mask to the outside world while leading normal active lives. But the truth is, they feel hopelessness and down. Sometimes even having thoughts about ending it all. Struggling with the strength to go on with their daily lives can make them especially vulnerable to conducting suicide plans. This contrasts with other forms of depression, in which people might have suicide ideas, but not enough energy to act on their intentions. Depression affects millions of people, more so now than ever, in these times of uncertainty. Please recognise that people have lives that we know nothing about and cannot comprehend.

We are aware of all the struggles in our own lives, but someone else could be carrying a heavier load. There are things that could have happened in someone's past or could be happening in their current lives that would completely change your view of them if you only knew. Every person has their secret sorrow which the world does not know, and often we call a person cold (or say they have an attitude, and you cannot stand them) when they are only sad and dealing with so much in secret. Let us be aware of how we treat people on the whole. There are so many things that you can intentionally do to make someone happy. The most important acts of kindness are those done in our everyday lives.

Respect other human beings whether you feel you are above them and they are beneath you, whether you are rich and they are poor, because I have heard those terms before. We should respect other human beings and treat them the same way we hope to be treated. Today, as you are blessed to receive the most precious gift of life and to see this amazing sunrise, be someone's ray of sunshine on a rainy day.

*And above all things have fervent charity among yourselves: for charity shall cover the multitude of sins. (1 Peter 4:8)*

Continue to take all the necessary precautions to keep yourself and family safe during these times of uncertainty. Stand still and let God move. When you feel you have reached the end and there is no way to go, just stand still and let God move.

Despite the challenges you may be experiencing, continue to shine your light for God. Continue to help others who may be going through similar situations like you. You will find joy and a purpose in your life through helping others. As a result, you will be inspired to promote your wellbeing onto the road of personal revival. Jesus sees beyond a broken person. God sees beyond our imperfections.

One of my nurses requested to go to Israel on holiday with her family. I told her it was not the correct time to go because too many people would have been on vacation at the same time. At first, she was not happy about the situation, but she settled for a different vacation date.

When she was preparing to travel to Israel, the war broke out. If she and her family had gone to Israel when she wanted to, they would have been caught up in Israel during the initial stages of the war. She told me she was happy that she and her family did not travel before, and she was happy that she changed her vacation dates. This nurse and her family were excited and told me they were going to the holy land. She then told me that the holy land had become a war zone. Sometimes God cancels our plans because only he can see what lies ahead. I was happy for that nurse that her vacation was changed to a later date. Due to the war, the nurse had to cancel her flight tickets.

Showing patience, kindness and love to those we encounter daily is particularly important. I think each person we meet is an opportunity of some kind. Even if we merely exchange a smile, it may leave an impression. Showing kindness can change someone's life in so many ways.

Family and friends are vital in maintaining a healthy emotional environment and wellbeing. Despite the unprecedented and uncertain times, there are still families and friends who do not communicate with each other.

The pandemic of COVID-19 was a terrible experience for millions of people. There were families and friends who did not see one another for years, yet people still have not learnt the true value of families and friends.

There are so many things happening in the world today. The Ukraine–Russia war where so many families were displaced. Families and friends were praying for months to see each other again. The Israel–Gaza war where so many people lost their lives and so many were displaced. So many were homeless and jobless. The Indian news where forty men were trapped for forty days. They did not know if they were going to see their families again. Thanks to the good Lord all forty men were rescued. They all made it out alive. There are people who only communicate with families and friends in troubled times or if something is needed. Why not let effective communication ensure a loving relationship unconditionally? It is a sad thing in the world today.

There are people who do not know about reunion because they do not believe in communicating with family and friends. A two-line message would not break a bone to say hello to someone who you have not reached out to for months or years. We are living in serious times, and we need to love our neighbours as ourselves. We need to look out for one another. Sometimes, if you never greet family members and friends, they will never greet you first. This is an incredibly sad thing today. Or sometimes you try to reach out to family and friends just for the sake of kindness and that message might be there for months unanswered. If you question it, the answer might be, "Oh, sorry, I was busy." Occasionally, people will call or send messages suddenly when it suits them. I usually respond. I will never say I am too busy.

Jesus asked, "Were there not ten that were healed? Where are the nine?" The daily messages in my inbox that I receive are mostly from strangers. Seldomly are they from family and friends. What a sad situation we are living in today.

I experience this on a continuous basis, but I have been inspired to share this message because I know you may be going through similar circumstances. Be strong and of good heart. God is our strength. The love of God is mighty to overcome any situation.

There is something beautiful in a reunion between families and friends that sometimes people do not understand. There are people who believe that their families and friends are here forever. Love one another. Be kind to one another. Love your neighbours as yourself. Find time for family and friends. Find time to help someone along the way. Find time to check up on family and friends. Even if it is just a two-line message as people do not like phone calls. People do not speak to their neighbours. People do not speak to their families and friends. People delay their blessings when they hold hatred, grudges and unforgiveness in their hearts. God created us all equal. No one is better than the other. It does not matter who you are or where you are from. It does not matter how rich you are or how big your house is or what car you drive or what job you have. We have learnt this over and over especially during the pandemic when money meant nothing, and God and family were our top priorities.

Let us stay humble and let love rule our hearts and minds because God himself is love. Every second you spend being unhappy, it is happy time wasted. When you feel everything is against you and you have no one to turn to and you do not know what to do, just give it all over to Jesus. He will turn your sorrows into joy.

For those of you who are broken-hearted today, keep your head high above the water. Keep your eyes on the higher prize, and Jesus' promise of joy coming in the morning will be yours.

If God wants to test you to see how strong your faith is in him, hang in there. Sometimes God does not take away all your problems at the same time. But sometimes we must smile in the face of problems. I did that for the past four years, and God has turned my problems to victories. Praise his name. I have asked God to grant me faith for future problems, as no one passes through this world problem-free. Sometimes we may smile, but our problems might be bigger than the problems of someone who cries about them.

Only a mighty God can give anyone peace to smile and comfort others when they themselves have problems. Anyway, please do not give up on God when you have problems. That is the time you need him more. God will never give up on you. So, never feel God is not there. It is either he is evaluating you, or you are the one who turned your back on him and treading into ungodly pastures. Have faith and put your trust in God. Even if money is not in your purse or wallet, it will be with you once you put your trust in God.

Personal revival of your life does not get better by chance, it gets better by change. There will never be enough time to do it right but find time to do it over. A person who dares to waste an hour of time has not discovered the value of life. Keep a little fire burning however small. There was never a night or a problem that could defeat sunrise or hope. Every morning is a new day with unfamiliar problems, but God gives us the knowledge to implement a solution. Keep your eyes on the Lord. Always remember each new morning God grants us all brand-new grace and mercies. We owe him all the thanks, honour, praise and glory for he is a great big wonderful God. It may seem like this world is ruling, but God is still in control. God is still on his throne.

You do not have to be positive all the time. It is perfectly okay to feel tearful, angry, annoyed, frustrated, scared and anxious. Having feelings does not make you a weak person. It makes you a human being. There is no normal life that is free of pain. It is the very wrestling with our problems that pushes us to grow. Not until we are lost do we begin to understand ourselves. You are not alone in this battle. God himself is commanding you today to be bold and courageous because, eventually, you will win this.

When our hearts are broken and we cannot see anything beyond our pain, it helps to remember God's promises to us. He promises to heal the broken-hearted and bind up their wounds. You may not see signs of that healing right now, but his promises are the same yesterday, today and forever. They are for all who believe. Healing is a process. It is not usually quick, easy or painless, but God is faithful. He promises he is near to the broken-hearted. He is pouring his strength into you at this very moment. He walks with you and goes before you. He is making a way where there seems to be no way. We have hope because of Jesus. He does not fail. What he promises will happen.

Swimming is more than just a physical activity; it is a powerful tool for enhancing mental and emotional wellbeing. Swimming can have a profound impact on our wellbeing. When we swim, our brains release feel-good chemicals like endorphins, which can help reduce stress and anxiety while boosting our mood. The rhythmic nature of swimming also promotes a meditative state, calming the mind. This can be especially beneficial for those dealing with mental health challenges. Additionally, the sensory experience of being in water can have a soothing effect on the nervous system, promoting relaxation and reducing symptoms of depression.

Swimming can also create a sense of accomplishment and self-esteem, as we set our minds for personal comebacks. The social aspect of swimming, when done in a group or team setting, can also provide a sense of community and support, further promoting our mental wellbeing. Swimming is not just about exercise; it is a holistic experience that nurtures both body and mind. Dive in and discover the transformative power of swimming.

Attending dancing classes also purify your mind and wellbeing. Dancing not only exercises your muscles, but it also improves our wellbeing and promotes our self-confidence. Dancing can be a joyful thing if you love dancing like I do. I am not talking about going to a dance party and so forth. I am talking about dancing at a concert, at a performance show, at a wedding or a friend's birthday party. It could be a dance group where you can meet up weekly. This will keep your mind away from depression.

Taking little walks or running sometimes can help you to overcome depression and help you on the road to recovery after failure or personal brokenness. If you love singing, try to join a choir group. Singing will bring joy to your soul and will build you back up quickly after a shattered life. Try to help others during your road to recovery. It will help you make a faster recovery. Your personal revival will be faster. God is the greatest.

Step out every day in faith knowing that you can do all things through Christ Jesus who gives you strength.

Do try to begin each day with a rainbow of joy in your heart. Let the rising sun paint a smile on your face. Remove all clouds of doubts and feel God's gift of a new day, new hope, new life, new opportunities and so many more blessings. Be a blessing to others each new day.

# Forgiveness

This is profound, divine and priceless. Forgiveness gives us a deep inner peace within our hearts.

You have a choice of staying away from the people who may have hurt you. Nevertheless, remember, forgiveness is one of God's given keys to happiness. To err is human and to forgive is divine.

Without the Holy Spirit in our lives, there is no forgiveness of sins. There will be no peace of mind for anyone if we do not let go of unforgiveness and forgive others, as God forgives us.

Have you ever noticed that people who hold grudges or don't forgive normally experience bad or poor health? Have you ever thought about the health significance of forgiveness?

Forgiveness improves our health. When we dwell on grudges, our blood pressure and heart rate spike. These are signs of stress which damage the body. When we forgive, our stress levels drop, and people who are more forgiving are protected from the negative health effects of stress. It can help free you from the control of the person who harmed you. Sometimes forgiveness might even lead to feelings of understanding, empathy and compassion for the one who hurt you. Forgiveness does not mean forgetting or excusing the harm done to you.

You will always have that feeling of separation from God if you fail to forgive others. You will have that feeling that you are in bondage to the power of evil or the power of sin. The more you struggle to escape or fight that feeling, the more it will remain dormant. The more you struggle, the more you realise you are helpless towards those feelings of an imprisoned mind. Your motives will be impure, and your heart will be unclean. For you to be set free from those horrible feelings, you need to forgive, so your heart and your mind can be cleansed from sin and be set free. Oh yes, unforgiveness is surely a sin.

Peace within is a divine action only God can give. Heaven's door will release the peace and joy your heart needs when you release your grudges and forgive. Even if you do not befriend the person anymore, the most important thing is that you need to free your mind from the hatred and the hurt and forgive, then you can move forwards with the peace of God within your beautiful heart.

One thing is for sure, money cannot buy forgiveness. Your education cannot buy it. Your wisdom cannot attain it. You can never hope by your own efforts to secure it. God can give it to you freely, even though forgiveness is priceless. It will be yours only if you decide to truly forgive others. God will forgive us of our sins if we ask him and truly repent from our sins. If we decline from forgiving others, God will not forgive us. You will always have that feeling of unhappiness in your heart. A clean and pure heart free from grudges, hatred and envy is so joyful. Why not try forgiving those who hurt you, then ask God to forgive you. This will be a miracle for your heart and mind.

It is a beautiful feeling when we forgive others. I know this because I have forgiven people repeatedly. The feeling of forgiveness is a wonderful feeling.

One of the beautiful seasons that people forgive each other is during the wonderful festive season of Christmas.

Speaking about the Christmas season, I am drafting this book in my small apartment in London, thanking God for the warmth of indoors during the winter season. It is December 2023 and God has been good. Sometimes I wonder about the people who struggle during the winter and have no place to live. I usually offer a pray for them. The church I attend provides night shelter for the homeless during the winter, as we need to be our brothers' and sisters' keeper. Sometimes they are unfortunate not to have any place to live during the winter.

God is merciful to us, so let us be merciful to others. God's grace and mercies are new each morning. To his name be praised and glorified. Thank God for life, yet another beautiful day, everyone, and everything.

Forgiveness is a powerful act of inner peace. When we forgive others, we not only grant peace to the people who wrong us, but we grant inner peace to ourselves.

Our families and friends may forsake us, but God will never forsake us. You may not be able to see those people you helped to climb the ladder anymore. Jesus said, "Were there not ten lepers cleansed? Where are the nine?" Only one person with leprosy returned to say thanks to the Lord. We see this every day of our lives today. Ungrateful hearts I call this. Gratefulness is divine in nature. It stemmed from the love of God within our hearts. Pray for those people who are ungrateful because they do not really know what they are doing. Unforgiving hearts are also something that can bring on physical illness. Forgiveness is divine because for one to forgive, the love of God must be within your heart.

Holding grudges for others is also another self-destructive agent. Invite God into your heart and life, entertain his love and that is the only way you will be able to drop the grudges, ungratefulness and unforgiveness. To err is human but to forgive is divine. Sometimes people may stop speaking to you without any reason. Count it as joy as sometimes God moves people away from our lives for a reason. People come into our lives for a reason and a season. When they leave, they will leave either a blessing or a lesson for us to learn and improve. In everything, give thanks and praise to almighty God for this is the will of God in Christ Jesus.

Parents are unable to speak to their children. Children are disrespectful to parents, aunts, uncles, teachers. We are living in serious times. Peer pressure is on the rise. Bible prophecies are happening.

It is never a good thing to return evil for good. The Lord will not be pleased with such conduct. Vengeance belongs to God. When we repay evil for good, it comes from a selfish heart. It compromises God's standards and is deserving of his judgement. Do you reward evil for good to those who show you kindness?

Let us be sure to reward good for good, instead of evil for good. We are told to: "love your enemies, bless them that curse you, do good to them that hate you, and pray for them which despitefully use you and persecute you." (Matthew 5:44) As children of God, we are to reward even those who did evil to us with good, leaving the reward of our behaviour towards them in God's hand.

If we do evil for those who did good to us, the Bible says that evil will not depart from our house. This conduct or behaviour is seen as brutish and wickedness in the sight of the Lord. Have you ever gone the extra mile for someone, only to have them reward you with evil? They may even judge your intentions or motives wrongfully because you are doing good.

However, we are assured that vengeance belongs to the Lord. Let us therefore be grateful to God for his goodness towards us. He loves us, cares for us, died for us and what do we do? We treat him with ingratitude. Let us listen and obey God. He will reward us by fighting our battles and seeking vengeance for us.

*Whoso rewardeth evil for good, evil shall not depart from his house. (Proverbs 17:13)*

Do not blame anyone who hurts you but instead thank God and learn a lesson. Life has much to offer even without certain people around you. God will still give you the people you need at each phase of life. Stop lamenting, stop crying, look at the windscreen and see the bigger picture. Focus on your journey so much that you do not have any space for negativity and use side mirrors only when you want to park for a while!

*Remember ye not the former things, neither consider the things of old. Behold, I will do a new thing; now it shall spring forth; shall ye not know it? I will even make a way in the wilderness, and rivers in the desert. (Isaiah 43:18–19)*

## Forgiveness

Do not hold onto anger. Someone once said that holding onto anger is like drinking poison and expecting the other person to die, and oh, how true that is for someone who does not know our loving God. Keeping all that bitterness and anger bottled up inside you will not hurt your enemy at all, but it will destroy "you" by robbing yourself of every ounce of happiness on this earth and in the earth to come, because you will not be there!

The Bible says: "For if ye forgive men their trespasses, your heavenly Father will also forgive you. But if ye forgive not men their trespasses, neither will your Father forgive your trespasses." (Matthew 6:14–15)

Nothing is worth missing heaven for, absolutely nothing, and certainly not something as miserable and oppressive as anger that just sucks the joy right out of your life! The only way to rid your soul of hatred and rage is to forgive.

You might say, "Well, it's just not that easy." The truth is, sometimes the hurt is so deep that it is just not humanly possible to forgive. But that is when you get on your knees and ask God to put his love and forgiveness in your heart for the person who caused you so much pain. You may not be able to love with "your love", but you can love with "God's love". So, reach out to Jesus and allow him to remove all anger, bitterness and revenge from your heart, and choose God's gift of joy! (Ephesians 4:31–32, Colossians 3:13, Luke 17:3–4 and 1 John 1:9)

God's grace is not only for certain people, but his grace is for us all. We are all under his saving grace. Our righteousness is like filthy rags before the sight of God and that's why God covers us with his glory and righteousness. Everything we do or say should be done to glorify the name of God and not the self.

If you are walking with the Lord, do not let anyone tell you about your past sins. Just say to them that your address has been changed. Glory be to God. Tell them you no longer live on Sin Street because God rewrote your life, and he has promoted you to salvation and Grace Street and you are living and walking in his favour. Hallelujah. Glory be to God.

When God sets us free from sins, our lives change for the better. The riches of this world should not be our goal. Our goal should be casting our eyes on that higher prize in Christ Jesus. Glory be to God. Hallelujah to the lamb of God. The riches of this world will strangely grow dim in the light of his glory and grace.

Thank you, Lord, for salvation so rich and so free. Love must be sincere. Hate what is evil. Cling to what is good. Be devoted to one another in love. Honour one another. Never be lacking in zeal, but keep your spiritual connection, serving the Lord. Be joyful in hope, patient in affliction, faithful in prayer. Share with those people who are in need. Practise hospitality. Bless those who persecute you; bless and do not curse. Rejoice with those who rejoice; mourn with those who mourn. Live in harmony with one another. Do not be proud but be willing to associate with people of a low position. Do not be conceited. Do not repay anyone evil for evil. Be careful to do what is right in the eyes of everyone. If it is possible, as far as it depends on you, live at peace with everyone. Do not take revenge, my dear friends and family, but leave room for God's wrath, for it is written: "Vengeance is mine; I will repay, saith the Lord. Therefore if thine enemy hunger, feed him; if he thirst, give him drink … Be not overcome of evil, but overcome evil with good." (Romans 12:19–21)

May the love of God and the fellowship of the Holy Spirit rest and abide with us all now and forever. Amen. Let the words of our mouths and the meditation of our hearts be accepted in thy sight, oh Lord, our strength and our redeemer. God loves you.

# Faith and Hope

These are two of the most powerful emotional mindsets we can have. Always embrace hope and faith, because it begins when you stand in the dark, looking out to the light. Faith is something that you and I need to go through life's situations. Faith is like climbing the stairs without seeing the steps, knowing that, whatever the situation is, God is there to guide and protect you.

There may be cases when you may be fighting hard with a bunch of keys to get a door open. In these cases, it could be the last key on the bunch that will open the door to remarkable success. Keep waiting in the hallway. Keep knocking on the door if you may. Keep praying and keep trusting God for deliverance. God will open that door to your success in perfect timing. Having faith continue in hope is a great gift from God. Those who hope in the Lord do not get distracted by the wavering events on Earth because they hope in the Lord for everything. We know every good thing comes from God. Faith and hope are strong, emotional and divine actions in the spiritual sense of the word.

Three Hebrew men were thrown in a furnace because they stood up for the truth. They knew whatever the outcome may be, they knew they served an almighty God. Instead of being burnt alive, the four men were seen in the fire dancing and praising God. Glory be to God.

Trusting in God, who is the author and the potter of your life, can retrieve any lost hope! You may not know how you made it this far were it not for God! Trust God in anything even when you do not understand.

That is how it will be when enemies try hard to destroy us. We shall rise above the storms because we serve a true and living God. The love of God is mighty and gives us the power to withstand the fiery darts of the evil one. Stand firm, brothers and sisters, family and friends. Our redeemer lives and he will stand with us in good and troubled times. Let us continue to give thanks and praise to the good Lord. The children of God shall receive the blessings of God, despite the challenges from enemies. When God says it, no one can stop his words from happening. This leaves me to say all glory, thanks, honour and praise to almighty God. We need to keep God alive in our hearts and minds knowing that, despite the unprecedented and uncertain times, God is still in control of everything and everyone. God is still the greatest.

I thank God for life, yet another beautiful day, everyone and everything. I pray that God's anointing and healing continue to touch every aspect of our lives. May the grace of God and the fellowship of the Holy Spirit rest and abide with us all now and forever. Amen. Let the words of our mouths and the meditation of our hearts be accepted in the sight of God, oh Lord, our strength and our redeemer. Amen. May the light and grace of the good Lord shine on us all and grant us all peace, comfort, happiness, strength and God's abiding love through Jesus' name. Amen.

Hope is like being in the dark looking out towards the light. Believe and trust in God. Pray and have faith in God that he will get you through the tunnel into the daylight.

In November 2023, forty men were trapped in an underground cave when it collapsed. They spent days trapped in there before they were rescued. All they had was faith and hope in God, believing that they would be rescued. They were indeed worried and fearful, not knowing if they were going to make it out alive. God came through for them by sending a particularly good rescue team, which exercised excellent skills. They were determined to save the men. The rescue mission ended with jubilation. Watching the news from my apartment in London, I was so overjoyed. I felt so happy as if I knew those men. The happiness on their faces was heartwarming.

Every day is a new beginning. God woke you up for a reason. His grace and mercies are new each morning. Take a deep breath, relax, give thanks, and praise and enjoy life's journey. It may seem cloudy now but have faith in God's timing. He will surely make a way for you.

Sometimes we complain of eating the same food often. We are tired of eating this and tired of eating that. What about the Israelites searching for the promised land who ate manna from heaven every day for forty years? They did not complain, and they could not complain because they did not have a choice. God fed them every day, and they were grateful and satisfied. Sometimes people waste food instead of taking the extra to homeless shelters. Sometimes we complain about wearing the same clothes or shoes. Have we ever thought about the homeless people who may be walking without shoes and in need of clothes? Let us be grateful and thankful to God for everything and help others whenever possible.

We sometimes complain about how hard our jobs are, but there are others who are searching for weeks, sometimes months, and cannot find a job. People do not speak to certain friends or family members, but there are people who do not have family or friends and are hoping to belong somewhere. There are people who may say their house is too small. What about those who are homeless? Have you ever thought about them for a second? How do they survive? Sometimes we think someone may be cold when they may only be sad. Try being kind to them. You may bring happiness to their soul.

## Faith and Hope

It is good to share our love, time, goods and kindness to everyone we meet. You never know, you may bring joy to someone's heart. Try it. God is with us.

Going into uncertainty and weathering the storm may be the only option for a resilient person. Courage is not having the strength to go on. It is going on when you do not have the strength. Life has difficulties. God did not promise us a smooth life. He promised to be there with us. Oaks grow strong in stormy winds and diamonds are made under pressure!

If you failed yesterday, dust yourself off and start again. Rome was not built in a day. It took years to build by diligent workers who had wonderful experience and great resilience.

There is hope for a tree. Even if you cut it down, it will sprout again, and its new shoots will not fail. Its roots may grow old in the ground and its stump may die in the soil, yet at the scent of water, it will bud and put forth shoots like a plant.

The very least you can do in your life is to figure out that for which you hope. And the most you can do is to live inside that hope. Just like the tree, you can hope for a brighter future. Just like the tree, you can rise again after falling.

Hope smiles from the threshold of the years to come, whispering, "It will be better for each new year, despite what you've gone through!" Hope can be a powerful force. There is no actual magic in it but when you know what you hope for most and hold it like a light within you, you can make things happen, like magic. They say a person needs just three things to be truly happy in this world: someone to love, something to do and something to hope for.

The very least you can do in your life is to figure out that for which you hope. And the most you can do is to live inside that hope. I will say that once we have the love of God within our hearts, we can hope for anything. We can have faith in God that anything is possible to those who believe.

Just like Joshua, we can ask God to do what seems impossible in human eyes. When God told Joshua that he would win the battle, Joshua told God that the sun would soon go down and the war was still raging. Joshua decided to trust God and asked him to hold back the sun, so he could finish the battle. Joshua had strong faith in God.

God did not only hold back the sun for hours, but he held it back until Joshua and his men finished the battle and won the war. Amen. Glory to God.

For us today, we can trust God to do the impossible for us too. Whatever the battle you are fighting today, I want to tell you our God can fight for us and win the war. Sickness, addiction, depression, homelessness, starvation, cancer, marital issues, same-gender relationships, anxiety, suppression. Whatever bondage you are under, I want to say that our God has already won the victory over everything. Our God is able. Trust him for everything. He parted the Red Sea, and he can make a way for you too.

Thank the good Lord for turning night into day. Thank him for everyone and everything. Thank you for Jesus Christ. We love you because you love us first and created us. Thank you for your saving grace. Thank you for your redeeming grace. Thank you for your healing power. Thank you for hearing and answering prayers through Jesus' name. Amen.

*Now faith is the substance of things hoped for, the evidence of things not seen. For by it the elders obtained a good report. Through faith we understand that the worlds were framed by the word of God, so that things which are seen were not made of things which do appear.*

*By faith Abel offered unto God a more excellent sacrifice than Cain, by which he obtained witness that he was righteous, God testifying of his gifts: and by it he being dead yet speaketh.*

*By faith Enoch was translated that he should not see death; and was not found because God had translated him: for before his translation he had this testimony, that he pleased God.*

*But without faith it is impossible to please him: for he that cometh to God must believe that he is, and that he is a rewarder of them that diligently seek him.*

*By faith Noah, being warned of God of things not seen as yet, moved with fear, prepared an ark to the saving of his house; by the which he condemned the world, and became heir of the righteousness which is by faith. (Hebrews 11:1–7)*

*Finally, my brethren, be strong in the Lord, and in the power of his might (Ephesians 6:10)*

When God breathes on your life, you will accomplish things that seem impossible. You will outlast opposition that should have overwhelmed you. You will discover talent and ability that you did not know you had. You will run and not be weary; you will walk and not faint.

You will ask, "Where did I get this strength?" It was God doing for you what he did for David, supercharging your life. Making things happen that you could not make happen.

God bless you.

# Failures

A winner is a dreamer who never gives up on what they are dreaming about. Despite discouraging days, you must press on if success is to be yours.

We should see all failures as stepping stones to victory. Anytime there is a failure, think about all your successes. This will help you to reduce the amount of emotional impact from your failure. This is not a terrible thing. It is only a disappointment and a delay on the road to success.

We all have had a physical fall or two at some point in our lives. Did we stay down where we fell? The answer is no. We often rise from where we fall. It is the same as when we have failures. We take the failure as a lesson learnt and we can look back and reflect on our mistakes. Once you know what the mistakes were, the lesson will equip you with the necessary knowledge to attain success in the future. Failures are stepping stones to improve your life, to take you on to succeed. You should never let failure stop you from your set goal.

Most great men and women achieved success after failures. Their accomplishments were achieved after discouraging hours. They made it to the top because they fought against those discouraging hours. They fought against failures. They did not give up. They fought against the struggle, and they never gave up. This is something that is difficult, but with motivation, persistence, resilience, hard work and prayer, the result is success. I know how difficult that is because I have been there and done that. I am happy that I never gave up on my dreams. That is another reason why I encourage everyone not to give up on their dreams. If I can do it, then anyone can do it. I do believe hope begins when you stand in the dark, looking out to the light.

Truth and error are close together. We need the Holy Spirit to stay on the path of truth. Giving up is not for the brave and noble men and women.

Do not blame anyone who hurts you but instead thank God and learn a lesson. Life has much to offer even without certain people around you. God will still give you the people you need at each phase of life.

Stop lamenting, stop crying, look at the windscreen and see the bigger picture. Focus on your journey so much that you do not have any space for negativity and use side mirrors only when you want to park for a while!

*Remember ye not the former things, neither consider the things of old. Behold, I will do a new thing; now it shall spring forth; shall ye not know it? I will even make a way in the wilderness, and rivers in the desert. (Isaiah 43:18–19)*

There are enemies who were set aside by God to play a role in our destiny.

*Be ye therefore perfect, even as your Father which is in heaven is perfect. (Matthew 5:48)*

God will accept only those who are determined to aim high. He places every human agent under obligation to do their best. Moral perfection is required of all. Never should we lower the standard of righteousness to accommodate inherited and cultivated tendencies to wrongdoing. We need to understand that imperfection of character is sin. All righteous attributes of character dwell in God as a perfect, harmonious whole, and everyone who receives Christ as a personal saviour is privileged to possess these attributes.

Let no one say, "I cannot remedy my defects of character." The real difficulty arises from the corruption of an unsanctified heart and an unwillingness to submit to the control of God.

Joseph would have never taken the throne without his brothers throwing him into the pit. David would have never become a king without facing Goliath. God would have never recognised and glorified in Babylon during the time of King Darius without Daniel being thrown into the lions' den. Jesus would have never risen from the grave and brought us salvation without Judas betraying him.

Stop worrying about who is not for you. Their chapter may be closed as part of your destiny. Therefore, I urge you today to keep running your race. Stop looking left or right; keep your focus and trust in God. If we could understand that enemies are keeping us in mind for failure but God is motivating us to reach our goals, we would never give up or become faint-hearted. If you keep on throwing a stone at every dog that barks at you, you will never reach your journey. Continue to shine your light.

There will be times when you may feel like quitting. Keep on dreaming and keep on praying. Keep on working towards your dream. Keep faith and hope alive. Believe in yourself and believe in God. Nothing is impossible.

It does not matter where you are now and what you are going through. Keep moving forward. People may think you cannot make it. Prove them wrong. Avoid gossip during your recovery process from failure.

In the rhythm of life's dance, let us take a moment to ponder something important. What if we actively sought out those tiny, everyday moments that stir our souls? Imagine facing challenges not as roadblocks, but as doorways to uncover strengths we did not know we had. And when we interact with others, let us genuinely embrace the uniqueness in each person because, honestly, nobody is a nobody. Every soul carries something special, a spark that makes the human experience so wonderfully diverse.

Think about those moments in your own life when unexpected inspiration struck or challenges turned into unexpected opportunities for growth. How did those experiences shape who you are and how you see the world?

Imagine inspiration as a treasure chest waiting to be discovered, just like the real-life experiences that shape our outlook. It takes a bit of courage to seek them out, but the profound wisdom gained often comes from those raw, personal moments. Your thoughts and stories in response to these musings are not just welcome, they are an essential part of the ongoing journey of life.

Where failure is a concern, giving up should not be an option. I encourage you to always keep moving forwards. People may ask, "How did you make it?" You should say that God helped you because you trusted him for your success. Helping others along your road to success is another way of moving forwards faster. If you do not move forwards, you will never know what is around the corner. You will never know what is over the fence. You will never know what is over the mountain. You will never know what is across the river. You will never know what is behind the walls or behind the rocks. Gold miners often gave up just before they reached the hidden treasure. Sometimes people work hard and give up just before they are about to gain success. This causes others to gain success at an easy attempt. This happened to the gold miners. They did not have to dig far for the gold due to others who gave up just before reaching the gold. Never stop trying.

Do you want to be in a situation where you wonder what it would have been like if you had pressed on longer? I guess not. It is always better to try and fail than not to try at all.

Just like the songwriter who says that you can get things if you really want. He went on to say that you just must try and try, and you will succeed at last. You just must keep trying. Beautiful oldies.

Please do not worry about falling sometimes. Just remember that you will be in an advantageous position to pray if you fall. With God guiding your life, you will rise from any fall with increased strength. It is not the fall that matters. It is how you rise that counts.

Any time I fall, I ask God to help me up. He always picks me up, touches me and gives me renewed strength to go on. He always plants my feet on higher ground. Praise God. Thanks and praise to almighty God.

Even if you have failures, remember God will not fail you. He promised to be there in enjoyable times and troubled times. Be not dismayed.

## Failures

I pray for faith, strength, peace, success, health, wealth, joy, love and happiness for myself, family, friends and others out there.

Knowledge is power and education is the key to success. Parents should ensure their children go to school to acquire knowledge to take them through life. Keeping children away from school without a proper reason is educational abuse. Also, the word of God tells us to train up our children in the ways of God and when they are older, they will not depart from such ways. God's ways are not always our ways. We must trust his will as he sees what lies ahead. Not every disappointment is something bad. Sometimes disappointments lead to something good.

One day, a local evangelist bragged during a crusade that his God was more able than all the other gods in the town and the powers of the universe the villagers worshiped put together. Just then, rainstorm sounds started sounding overhead, threatening the progress of the crusade. The evangelist lifted his voice and declared with confidence that if the rain fell, then he was not a man of God; he would stop preaching!

Before he could finish his bluff, the rain began to hit the crusade grounds so vehemently in disregard to his declarations. The whole town left the crusade grounds to their houses, shaking their heads in disappointment and dismay.

The evangelist, so distraught and angry, packed his belongings and left the town the next day. On his way through the next town, he checked into a local drinking spot and drank himself into a stupor. As he lay on the ground cursing God, an old seedy-looking man tapped him gently on the shoulder.

"Man of God..." the old man began.

The evangelist quickly cut in. "Don't mention the name of God to me. He is fake. He is unreliable. I am no longer a believer in this God. A God who chooses to disgrace his servants. Leave me alone!"

But the old man would not let him be. He continued. "I am the fetish priest in the village you just preached at. During your one-week stay in that village, you destroyed all the charms I had made on the people for forty-five years. Your prayers and your words always came with fearful fire and power. I tried so many times to eliminate you, but I could not. My last chance came yesterday. I loaded my gun with gunpowder and lay in wait on the mountaintop where I had a noticeably clear view of you. My plan was to shoot you from a distance since I could not get close enough to you due to the fire around you. But just when I lifted the gun, the rain came from nowhere, wetting my gunpowder and covering you in a cloud so that I could not even see you. All I saw was a bright man holding a sword in front of you. I was so terrified. I concluded that your God was indeed all powerful and almighty. That is why I have been looking for you since then. I want to follow your God!"

The ex-evangelist bowed his head in shame!

Dear friends and family, sometimes it is wise for us to believe that our Lord knows the way he is taking us. We should just trust his leading. Let our boast be in the Lord, not in ourselves. If we decree a thing and it does not happen, let us not see it as disappointment or dishonour from the Lord. Let us just believe that the Lord wants his perfect will to be done in all things. We never lose battles. We either gain something from it or learn lessons.

Nobody can successfully be against you if God is on your side. God is the greatest captain anyone can ever rely on in times of trouble, difficulty and battle. Romans 8:31 asked: "What shall we then say to these things? If God be for us, who can be against us?" The answer is no one.

If Christ Jesus is on your side, you do not need to fight the battles because he will fight for you. Is Jesus Christ on your side? If not, ask him to come to you and take over your battles by simply surrendering to him. My prayer for you today is that you may always call on God to help fight your battles. He is a God of victories.

Stop worrying too much about what you were not able to do! Worry never accomplishes anything. When you have a problem, it is best to concentrate on the solution to that problem, not the problem itself. Always remember that being challenged in life is inevitable, but being defeated is optional. Dust yourself off and keep going.

# Personal Revival

It is only in our darkest hours that we may discover the true strength of the brilliant light within ourselves that can never ever be dimmed. We either make ourselves miserable or we make ourselves strong. The amount of work is the same. The choice is yours!

We sustain a loss when we neglect the privilege of associating together to strengthen and encourage one another. If we show love to one another and help strengthen each other, our own hearts will be refreshed.

*Now the God of hope fill you with all joy and peace in believing, that ye may abound in hope, through the power of the Holy Ghost. (Romans 15:13)*

A miracle happens every single day of your life. You are given the opportunity to live another day and to experience what the world has to offer, and that is something you must always remember and appreciate. Be grateful and be thankful. The love of God within our hearts will grant us that personal revival.

*But they that wait upon the Lord shall renew their strength; they shall mount up with wings as eagles; they shall run, and not be weary; and they shall walk, and not faint. (Isaiah 40:31)*

Hope begins when you stand in the dark, looking out to the light. Personal revival begins with hope.

To be fully revived, one needs to have acceptance of the brokenness with oneself. The next stage is to pray and ask God to take full control of your life. Allow God to direct your life and pour revival ideas into your thoughts. Do not dwell on the past. Any past mistakes cannot be redone, but you can move forwards to a brighter future. Think about the things that truly make you happy, instead of thinking about your past. Practise letting your thoughts focus on only positive things. Do not allow negative thoughts to control your mind because this will delay you on the road to recovery.

As a man was riding along in his Ford, suddenly something went wrong. He got out and looked at the engine, but he could find nothing wrong. As he stood there, another car came in sight, and he waved it down to ask for help.

Out stepped a friendly man who asked, "Well, what's the trouble?"

"I do not know. There is something wrong with the engine," he replied.

God is an author, and the potter of your life can retrieve any lost hope. You may not know how you made it this far were it not for God. Enemies are everywhere but you still navigate, blessing after blessing. A man who keeps looking up for help is hard to beat. Trust God in anything at your worst and you will enjoy everything at your best!

God made you and me, and he alone knows how to run your life and mine. We would make a complete wreck of our lives without Christ. When he is at the controls, all goes well. Without him, we can do nothing.

Just like night and day operates in shifts, certain people are going to leave your life, but that is not the end of your story. That is the end of their part in your story. I will always encourage you to look up and bank your hopes in God. He repairs the bleeding hearts and gives a new name even to the poor!

*But they that wait upon the Lord shall renew their strength; they shall mount up with wings like eagles; they will run, and not be weary; they will walk, and not faint. (Isaiah 40:31)*

It is a good thing to help others in need during the time you yourself are in need. It is also a good thing and a fruitful experience to help others who are broken and aching from one thing or another. Helping people when you yourself are broken is a powerful way of reviving yourself from brokenness. This is another step of moving away from the path of emotional brokenness onto the road to personal revival. I have learnt repeatedly from personal experience that helping others in my dark moments gave me inner joy.

Sometimes when I gave freely and generously, people would joke and say I was rich. I have proven in my life that to give freely brings joy to my life. Remember, we give not to receive, but we give expecting that the good Lord will bless us in return. Giving to others and showing love to others is an act of the love of God within our hearts. Love is powerful. Giving to others is also a powerful act of kindness. This gives inner peace, joy and satisfaction to the heart. When someone can give and care for others when they themselves are in need, it shows that the love of God is allowing that person to show love for others. These acts of kindness will help anyone overcome any form of brokenness. Get your life back in order by taking care of yourself and helping others who need help.

I know of people who counselled people when they themselves needed counselling. By doing so, they were able to motivate themselves into a faster recovery process.

We may pass someone on the road, and they might give you a half smile. Try to smile back at that person. Give them a full smile and you can give kind words. I notice that most people who have given me a half smile were not happy. I smiled at those people, gave them some kind words, then I saw a full smile after those kinds of words. Sometimes we assume people are unkind if they have a serious face. People may assume they are cold or unkind, when in fact they may need help in so many ways. They may need emotional help. They may need financial help. When communicating with people, you may be surprised to know the things people have gone through or are still going through. Yet, we see them walking the streets as if nothing is wrong.

There are homeless people, and we may not know. This is because there are people who still walk the road looking neat and tidy. They might use public facilities to tidy up. There are people who do not have a job. Or they might have a small job and still nowhere to live. There are so many people who are aching from one thing or another. Sometimes people will open up to you about their struggles. There are people who may keep their struggles hidden. They are broken emotionally, and we may not know because of their silent hidden life.

I am amazed at how people who are trying to help themselves out from these situations still try to help others. Freely give, freely receive. I do believe that people can motivate themselves during the process of personal revival, especially if you put God first in everything you do. God will find a way out for you. If God can open a fountain in the wilderness, he can turn your life fully around from your situation.

Only God can turn a mess into a message, a test into a testimony, a trial into a triumph, a victim into a victory and a problem into a prayer.

Rise and shine and give God all the thanks and praise once you rise and see the dawn of this new day. Hallelujah. Praise God, there are new mercies. It is a miracle. It is a new day with new mercies. Be thankful to the almighty God.

Put all those problems and heartaches behind you. Give them over to the Lord. God gives Jesus the authority to be the mender and healer of all your broken dreams. I have proof of what I am talking about. If God can do it for me, he can do it for you.

Turn around and investigate the path God wants you to go. Take his hands and hand over all your problems to him. Problems do not always last.

I always believe that rain does not fall forever, and the storms always pass over. There is always a silver lining. Therefore, when you see the darkest hour approaching, put a smile on your face, as you will know the dawn will soon be in sight.

When you pray, God listens. It is good to work hard along with prayer. When you listen, God talks, and he works on your behalf.

God loves you and me, so get rid of those problems. Enjoy life to the fullest and ask God for his peace that will give you that joy, that money, that the world cannot give.

I wish us all God's grace, peace and joy as we go through this beautiful day he has made. Let us rejoice and be glad in it. Keep pressing on and you are going to make it. You will do great and beautiful things with God on your journey of life.

Please do not let the turbulence of life distract you into thinking that the odds are against you. You are a champion. You are a star in your own stories. You are a hero.

No matter what is happening around you in the natural realm, you have God's favour on your side. You have God's grace each new morning. You are blessed and highly favoured beyond measure in your going out and your coming in.

Look around you and around the world at large, and you will see what is going on. Then you will be able to confirm how blessed you are. You will attract beautiful things everywhere you go. Remember, you are beautiful and wonderful, and made by the great creator almighty God. You were created as a masterpiece by the king of all kings and lord of all lords. He is the great creator.

Keep your thoughts positive, as they will generate positive feelings and attract positive life experiences. To be happy, you must make yourself happy, so you can make others happy. Remember, you are not alone. Look around you and know that you are loved. Even if you feel alone, the Lord is there with you.

I am sitting in my London apartment writing this book. It is winter 2023 and I thought, *Why not write something about Christmas in this special chapter?*

The Christmas spirit is about giving. The Christmas spirit is about love, which should be shown all year round. The Christmas spirit is about forgiveness. Lights of assorted colours have something to do with boosting people's spirits and they bring joy to our hearts. I love the beautiful lighting up at Christmas time. Despite the chilly weather at Christmas time, the Christmas lights help to brighten up the dullness from the cloudy and damp weather. Christ Jesus is the reason for the season, and he gives us joy in our hearts.

Inspiration should never be expensive. Remember to share your goods with those in need. In saying this, I must remind you that it does not matter the love and help you think you are giving out. If you do not love your neighbours, it is simple. You do not love God. If you do not love your siblings, it is saying that you do not love God.

There is hope for a tree. Even if you cut it down, it will sprout again, and its new shoots will not fail. Its roots may grow old in the ground and its stump may die in the soil, yet at the scent of water, it will bud and put forth shoots like a plant.

The very least you can do in your life is to figure out that for which you hope. And the most you can do is to live inside that hope. Just like the tree, you can hope for a brighter future. Just like the tree, you can rise again after falling.

Hope smiles from the threshold of the years to come, whispering, "It will be better for each new year, despite what you've gone through!" Hope can be a powerful force. There is no actual magic in it but when you know what you hope for most and hold it like a light within you, you can make things happen, like magic. They say a person needs just three things to be truly happy in this world: someone to love, something to do and something to hope for.

The very least you can do in your life is to figure out that for which you hope. And the most you can do is to live inside that hope. I will say that once we have the love of God within our hearts, we can hope for anything. We can have faith in God that anything is possible to those who believe.

Consider everyone you meet a blessing. No one is your enemy. Anyone who annoys you is teaching you patience and calmness. Anyone who abandons you is teaching you how to stand up on your own feet. Anyone who offends you is teaching you forgiveness and compassion. Anything you hate is teaching you unconditional love. Anything you fear is teaching you courage to overcome your fears. Anything you cannot control is teaching you to let go. When people keep refusing to help you, it is teaching you to be independent. When you are facing problems one after the other, this is teaching you how to get a solution to problems. When people attack you, this is teaching you the best form of defence. Anyone who looks down on you is teaching you to look up to the creator almighty God.

Always look out for the lesson in every situation you face in every phase of life. Be polite, calm, gentle and thankful to God because he will be with you to the end. Life had taught me lessons. I do not see people at my crossroads because humans are not dependable. I only see God as the author and finisher of my faith.

When you live your life without anyone betraying, hurting, disappointing, disgracing or offending you, then it means you never did anything worthy. *

The beauty of life is that it comes with disappointments and betrayals from people you least expect. Unfortunately, sometimes we spend so much time crying over these betrayals and disappointments, we end up becoming victims of all circumstances. *

Remember one thing, holding onto anger is like knocking your head on a wall and expecting the other person to feel the pain. You are only hurting yourself.

The fact is, the world is full of annoying, naughty, stupid and ungrateful people, and you will always come across them at one point or another in life. But the best thing to do is deal with them with wisdom and maturity. You cannot get everyone to love you, think like you or behave like you. We must learn to tolerate and overlook certain things; we must try to bury the faults of others and move on with life.

Anger, hatred and intolerance have caused the world's problems and solved none. Life is short. You do not know how much more time you have left.*

I beseech you to take the pain and forgive that special person you hold grudges against, and iron out your grievances. Muster the courage and apologise to that person you have offended. *

The amount of money or number of houses and companies you have do not measure the life you have. Your life is measured by the positive impact you have made in the lives of others.

Sometimes a rainbow can be seen after the storm. Trouble and trials will come, but remember these do not last always. A miracle happens every single day of your life. You are given the opportunity to live another day and to experience what the world has to offer, and that is something you must always remember and appreciate. Be grateful and be thankful.

May God continue to richly bless us all as we continue to trust him for our holistic growth.

The act of giving and sharing is a way to overcome brokenness. This will help you with personal revival. I have learnt to give and share not because I have much but because I know how it feels to have nothing. I have also learnt that a person can have everything and still not have happiness. Giving brings joy to the hearts of people.

# Success

Most great men and women achieved success after failures. Their accomplishments were achieved after discouraging hours. They made it to the top because they fought against those discouraging hours. They fought against failures. They did not give up. They fought against the struggle, and they never gave up. This is something that is difficult, but with motivation, persistence, resilience, hard work and prayer, the result is success. I know how difficult that is because I have been there and done that. I am happy that I never gave up on my dreams. That is another reason why I encourage everyone not to give up on their dreams. Thank God for his grace and mercies which are new each morning.

Please remember that your present circumstances do not determine your destiny. It determines where you start. The sun is weak when it rises and increases in strength as the day goes on. You do not have to be great to start somewhere, but you must start from somewhere to be great. There are opportunities every single day. Sometimes opportunities never resurface. Grab hold of opportunities when you have the chance.

Remember, limitations live only in our minds, but if we use our imaginations, our possibilities become limitless. Things will get better one day. Cling to that hope! May God's favour continue to be our portion as we continue to trust him with our life and our destiny, as God holds the future.

Shoot for the moon. Even if you miss, you will land amongst the stars! It is better to aim high and miss, rather than to aim low and hit. Get a bigger dream. You have something special. You have greatness within you because a great big wonderful God created you.

In every heartache, remember your worth. Tough times do not define you; they refine you. Embrace the journey for you were destined for greatness. Your struggles are temporary; your endurance is eternal. Keep working, praying and believing. Your life is a canvas. Paint it with resilience, positivity and hope. Your story is still unfolding, and brighter chapters await you. Embrace hope.

God does not choose the qualified to do the work. He chooses the unqualified and qualifies them to do the tasks. The disciples were ordinary people and they became great men sharing the gospels of Christ.

The gospels are real stories with real people. Just like us today, our stories are real and will be for future generations to come. Let our stories be the kind that future generations will be proud of and stories of good examples. Always remember you and I are heroes within our own stories. Let our stories be pleasing in the sight of God. Let our stories motivate others and not offend them. Let us not only speak about doing good, but let us demonstrate the good we speak about. We should believe in ourselves and stop doubting that we will be able to make it.

Allow the good Lord into your life. This will be a time when your blessings will be with overflow. Do not forget to share your blessings with others. I always believe that helping others is a way of helping ourselves. Remember, we give not to receive, but we give expecting God to bless us in return.

Look in the mirror if you would like to know who is responsible for a percentage of your troubles. People suffer because of their actions, wrong decisions, behaviours and disobedience. The kind of life you live today will be manifested tomorrow.

The Bible says: "For whatsoever a man soweth, that shall he also reap." (Galatians 6:7) When you live according to the faith of Christ Jesus, you will be destined for a perfect tomorrow. God is perfect. My decree today is that you will sow according to God's pattern and purpose in Jesus Christ. Amen. Arise and shine for thy light has come.

*Remember ye not the former things, neither consider the things of old. Behold, I will do a new things; now it shall spring up; shall yet not know it? I will even make a way in the wilderness, and rivers in the desert. (Isaiah 43:18–19)*

Sometimes you fail to notice that you are walking the life you once dreamt of because somehow in between, you shifted your desires to goals that are beyond your current ability. You may sometimes surround yourself with people who may cause you to drift off track from your goals. You may focus more on what others are doing more than focusing on what you are aiming to do. You may be surrounded by opportunities you wished to have, but you are so used to them that you look at them as ordinary things.

One of the greatest comebacks you can achieve is making yourself happy by acknowledging the steps you have made so far. Never forget the battles God has fought on your behalf. You may not be there yet, but persist in your struggles. Rome was not built in a day. Your victory will take time. Just remain focused on your journey towards your dream goal.

Do not confuse your path with your destination. Just remember to keep focused and keep on track. Just because it is stormy now does not mean you are not heading for sunshine. Behind every dark cloud is a silver lining.

The biggest obstacle to moving forwards is fear. People are afraid to think big, but if you think small, you will only achieve insignificant things. Again, remember that the day you stop doing the trivial things is the day you think you are above everybody else. For the person for whom insignificant things do not exist, the great is not great. Just begin small today…

Be incredibly careful how you live. Not as unwise but as wise, making the best of every opportunity, because the days are evil. Take advantage of new opportunities to strengthen your faith and create meaningful connections in your everyday life. And when life gives you the opposite, sing like no one is listening, love like you have never been hurt, dance like nobody's watching and live like it's heaven on Earth!

Do not pray for easy lives. Pray to be stronger men and women. Do not pray for tasks equal to your powers. Pray for powers equal to your tasks. You shall sometimes wonder about the richness of life which has come to you by the grace of God.

Do not carry your mistakes around with you. Place them under your feet and use them as stepping stones. If the stepping stones lead you to success, then that is good. If they do not, then use them as experience.

Remember, when you succeed in life, try to remain kind to everyone. Do not let money change your character.

Rich or poor, we should have the same kind and loving character. When I had little, I shared. When I have, I share.

I know that due to the uncertain and unprecedented times which are on us, people are getting frustrated, and sometimes people think about giving up. Giving up should not be an option. My motto is never give up. Always aim for the moon. If you fall, you will land between the beautiful stars.

People with weak hearts and weak minds give up easily, not knowing if they had pressed on a little longer they would have experienced success. This happened to gold miners who gave up and other gold miners visited the same site and accomplished remarkable success because of perseverance. Motivation, determination and perseverance are key to attaining enormous success. Once we put into action what our hearts and minds tell us, we can achieve those goals.

I had discouraged hours and failures in life, but I took them as stepping stones to success. Just like me, you can use your discouraging hours and failures to set future goals. We learn from our mistakes and failures as these are great lessons to help promote us to success.

If your plan does not work, try another action plan which will lead you to your goals. It is the same as taking a taxi or a bus if the train workers are on strike. Try all means to get to your destination safely. In that same way, we should try hard to get to our goals with remarkable success. The beauty of success is being your best in whatever you do. In failures, frustration or discouraging hours, say a prayer. Do something you like to do. Visit friends and family. Sing a song you like. Watch a funny movie. Try to think about people who have gone through worse times than you. These things will help you to understand that your situation could have been worse. Helping others who need your support will help you to motivate yourself. Sharing your experiences with others will help you to release your unhappy feelings towards your failures.

Keep hope alive. Continue to think positively knowing there is always light at the end of the tunnel. Continue to look up and work hard towards your goals in life. Do not let anyone tell you that you cannot make it in life. With God in your life, nothing is impossible. Keep pressing on to your goals. That is why I love to watch the Athletics Championship games. Sometimes athletes are seconds away from winning the gold. I love when this happens. This tells us that sometimes we are just seconds away from reaching our dreams that will give you the career arena you have been dreaming about. People may laugh at you and say you cannot make it. This may get you down but continue to move on towards your goals in life.

I love victories. I love success. I love celebrations. I love getting through that stage of hearing "well done" or "congratulations". You are thinking the same. I use a brief word of prayer before I embark on any goal in life.

During the COVID-19 pandemic, I mentioned to my daughter Crystal that I would write my first book and get it published in 2023. I can remember my daughter looked at me and smiled. She supported me as she told me she loved the inspirational messages I wrote on Facebook. That made me feel motivated. Then she said, "I know you will draft a nice book, but I am not sure if people will buy your books as mostly celebrities and rich people are popular in book selling."

I laughed it off. I got a bit discouraged, but my daughter said, "But you can still write your book as I am sure people will buy your books."

I told her I knew of people who wrote books but who were not rich or celebrities and they made it in the industry. Crystal said, "Okay, Mum, it is true. Go for it."

In 2021/2022, I wrote my first book *Valley to the Mountain: Blessings and Lessons.* This book was published on 6 March 2023, and it is non-fiction.

In 2022/2023, I wrote my second book *Faith in God: Unseen Steps to Victory.* This book was published on 12 May 2023.

From February to April 2023, I wrote my third book on weekends and nights called *Professional Excellence: Education Is the Key.* This book was published in September 2023.

I have just completed my fourth book called *My Journey as a Nurse: Noble Profession*.

I am not perfect, and no one is but God. If I can write four books and I do not have a broad experience in writing books, then you too can attain anything you want to do once you put your heart, your soul and your mind into it. Writing can become addictive if you love writing like I do. This is my fifth book, and I am enjoying writing.

God did not promise us a smooth life all the time, but he promised to be there to protect us and guide us through. The same with the roads you drive on. There are smooth roads and there are bumpy roads. When you reach the bumpy spots on the roads, you drive slowly and carefully. Your car will break down sometimes, but you do not leave it on the road. You will get it fixed. It is the same with going for gold. When we fall, we do not stay down. We must get up, brush off and keep going. The race is not always for the swift but for all those who endure to the end. In the recent Athletics Championship games, I saw someone was coming first in the race. She fell three seconds before the finish line and the person who was second touched the finish line first. Oh yes, these things happen often. Stay on course. Keep looking at the finish line. Focus on the finish line. Do not look at what anyone else is doing. Focus on your dream goal or goals. I love the saying "going for gold". I also love the part of getting the goal. We all do for ourselves, our families and our friends.

Dreams were meant to be accomplished. Let your dreams become reality. Please never give up as I always say giving up should not be an option. Keep on going to the finish line to get your goals.

Do not measure your success by your possessions. Success could be accomplished by so many things you do to bring joy to the lives of others. A ray of sunshine shining through the trees in the forest will give the hunters joy in their hearts that there is no sign of rain on the way.

That is how our life is. It does not matter how terrible things might seem sometimes, there is always hope and a ray of sunshine. Have faith. Keep hope alive. The sun will eventually shine through fully in your lives. God is good.

I also love the movie *The Sound of Music* and I love the song "Climb Ev'ry Mountain". The song is saying that we should climb every mountain, ford every stream, follow every rainbow until we find our dream. If you are determined to accomplish your dreams, keep moving forwards. If you reach a closed road, pray and ask God for another direction. Sometimes discouraging hours may lead to greater success if you have faith and hope.

Every woman who walks with God has a story to tell. Remember, before the glory, there must be a story. If you talk to Sarah, she will tell you nothing is too hard for God to do. If you talk to Haggai, she will tell you even in the wilderness God is still there. If you talk to Rahabu, she will tell you God can use anything and anyone at any time. If you speak to Hannah, she will tell you her God answered her prayers. If you talk to Ruth, she will tell you it is not over until God says it is over. If you talk to Esther, she will tell you God can turn a nobody into a somebody. If you talk to Elizabeth, she will tell you that you can carry and give birth to greatness. If you talk to Mary, she will tell you let it be onto you according to the word of God.

If yesterday you were able to walk only one mile, that was impressive. Do not give up. Keep going. Use yesterday as an inspiration for today's success. May the almighty God rewrite your story and turn your sorrows into joy through the mighty name of Jesus Christ. Amen.

# Giving Thanks

Simply saying thank you to someone is a special thing. Most of the time, those with the least give more generously. Saying thanks and giving thanks by gratitude or appreciation can be done in so many ways, which is a priceless treasure. Buying a thank you gift for someone is an effective way of showing your gratitude. Inviting someone at lunchtime to say thanks is something beautiful.

There are people who do not know what please and thank you are. These two words are extremely important and powerful. Most people are grateful when you say please and thank you.

It does not matter what you went through or what you are going through, continue to give thanks and praise to God. The act of thanks and praise always generates a positive divine energy that promotes our spiritual wellbeing. This brings us closer to God in the spiritual realm. Even though God may not answer our prayers when we want him to, rest assured he is moving to answer and deliver at the right time. God is never early in answering our prayers. He is never late in answering our prayers, but God always answers our prayers in his own perfect timing. He is always right on time because he is a God of perfection. When we pray, we just need to stand still, relax, trust in God and allow him to answer our prayers when he is ready. It may not be the answer you and I are looking for, but God's answers are always the best answers. This is because he holds the future in his hands, and he knows what is best for us at any given time. Let God be our daily devotion agenda.

Have you ever taken your time and counted the blessings God has given to you? God has endowed us with things we forget to appreciate. Instead, we complain, and our hearts grow faint of what we do not have. Nobody pleases and receives more from God than a person with a thankful heart. A thankful heart attracts more blessings from God. People become unhappy and unsatisfied because they think about what they have not got. Count what you have, not what you do not have.

*He that is faithful in thatIch"is l'ast is faithful also in much: and he that is unjust in the least is unjust also in much. (Luke 16:10)*

When you are faithful with the little you have, God will be faithful to give you more. If you do not give thanks and enjoy what you have, how could you be thankful and happier with more? We must be thankful. For example, your breath. My plea for you is that always thank God and he will do more for you. Do we have to wait until Christmas for a miracle? The answer is no. We receive a miracle from God every morning we wake up to see another beautiful day. Sun or rain, God beautifully creates every day.

Do we have to wait until Christmas to do charitable deeds and love our neighbours as ourselves? The answer is no. We should show love to everyone and do virtuous deeds throughout the year. Doing charitable deeds is another way of saying thanks to God for his love and kindness towards us. Putting God first above everyone and everything is demonstrating your love for God. It is also saying thanks to God for his goodness towards us.

When we accomplish our goals and success is showing on our faces, let us remember to invite God into our celebrations by first saying thanks to him.

I do things for others, and sometimes they fail to return a message to say thanks. I sometimes feel bad about it, but I try not to let the simple things of life get me down. The peace and joy of God will help us to overcome such things.

In the Bible, it mentions the story of the ten people with leprosy. Jesus healed them. They all were excited and ran away rejoicing. Only one returned to Jesus to say thank you. Jesus asked him, "Were there not ten of you? Where are the nine?" This happens in our society. People sometimes forget to say thanks. They might apologise and say they were busy.

In my life, I encountered various challenges, but God has been good. I overcame those challenges because God is a faithful and good God. Failures and disappointments meant something in various aspects. I learnt lessons from them, and sometimes they were experiences that taught me how to overcome the other disappointments. Those failures and disappointments were stepping stones to success.

I worked as a registered nurse manager for eight years but worked in nurse management for fourteen years. I have been a nurse for forty-two years. In my fourteen years of nurse management, I had about ten CQC inspections under my management. My workplace failed one inspection, two were "required improvements" and seven were rated "good". I could not have done that without God on my side.

I worked as a registered manager for about eight years. In those eight years, I had seven inspections under my management. One was a failed inspection but I overcame that with seven rated "good". Again, without God on our side, this would not have been possible.

The last CQC inspection was in November 2023, and we were rated overall "good". I have decided to resign knowing that for more than five years my workplace was rated overall "good" and it was time to move on to other aspects of my life. It is a great feeling and blessing to have been able to manage a sixty-four-bed nursing care home for eight years and maintain an overall "good" rating. Glory goes to God. Thanks to all the staff, the visiting professionals, the families and the residents who also helped to make this possible.

I ended my working journey at the care home on 18 December 2023. I was given a heartwarming farewell get-together on 15 December followed by another farewell get-together with the CEO and the director of the company. It was an amazing experience and an amazing journey. My registered manager journey started on my birthday eight years ago and ended with a beautiful get-together. I welcomed the great heartwarming speech, beautiful cards, gifts, flowers and money.

You would never believe this was the same nurse and midwife who passed through failures and disappointments. The good thing is, I never gave up because I do not believe in giving up.

Enjoying the time off from work feels strange but it is time to have time away from the hustle and bustle of working life. Going back to teaching is an idea that came to mind, but I will see what God has in store.

In the meantime, I will continue to write and do what I love to do. Attending church worship, prayer meetings, choir practice and Bible study keep me busy in the meantime. Along with shopping, cooking, cleaning and watching movies, you name it. Chatting with family and friends is a daily chore for me as family and friends are a vital part of life.

# Reasons for Writing This Book

I love writing inspirational messages to family, friends and others out there. I have been writing these messages on various social media platforms for years. I received feedback from people regarding my messages. People were inspired and motivated by my messages. There are people who sometimes send me messages asking me to pray for them. I also preached in church twice, so I thought writing my messages in a book would be good for others to read.

It was also suggested to me by a friend Sahai that I should write an inspirational book. She said she liked the inspirational messages I sent to her. Sahai encouraged me to write a book on inspirational quotes.

We are living in unprecedented and uncertain times. This book, about faith and hope and so much more, will inspire and uplift people.

There are millions of people out there who are suffering from depression and this book will help them to cope better, especially the three chapters "Storm Clouds", "Brokenness" and "Personal Revival". The other chapters are also inspiring. The term "mental health" is prevalent, as our young people are suffering from various forms of mental health issues. I have seen people who had challenging times recovering from diverse types of addiction such as alcohol addiction. These people need our help. Simply speaking to these people can help lighten the load of what they are feeling and going through.

Millions are homeless, of which we know not about, because they are ashamed and good at covering it up. If you happen to know of someone who is homeless, and you believe they are hiding the fact, seek help for them. Or you can direct them to the appropriate authorities.

I named my book *A Ray of Sunshine*. This is because sometimes people believe that when they are in the stormy days, they do not have the faith that the storm will ever be over. They are so broken that they do not believe that their lives could ever get back on track. I also wrote about faith and hope because I would like for others to exercise more trust in faith and hope. Keep hope and faith alive.

My book also touches on failure and success. I wanted to have these in my book because so many people have mental health issues due to failures leading to brokenness. When it is difficult for people to recover from failure, they sometimes turn to drugs and other self-harming things.

After the storms of life, failures and brokenness, we will be able to help others on the road to personal recovery. The chapter on success will also help those who went through failure to be able to pick themselves up and be able to climb the ladder to success again.

At the end of the day, failure does not determine your goals in life. Picking yourself up after failure and getting yourself to the finish line is what determines your destiny. Pray and trust God to get you to the finish line of your goal.

My book is teaching others that failure does not mean the end of your dreams. People who are in remarkably high positions in the academic arena could say how difficult it was for them too.

# Book Summary

In my chapter "Storm Clouds", I wrote about a ray of sunshine. When you have a ray of sunshine in your heart, you will continue to keep hope alive. Your dawn shall come.

I believe that rain does not fall forever, and storm clouds always pass over. I believe there is light at the end of every tunnel. As the saying goes, behind every dark cloud, there is a positive aspect, or a silver lining. Sometimes a rainbow can be seen after the storm. Trouble and trials will come, but remember these do not last always.

This book will give you emotional support when life is not going as you would like it to go. We should believe in ourselves and stop doubting we will be able to make it.

When life throws lemons at you, make lemonade. Selling lemonade for years can make you rich. What I am trying to say is that it does not matter where you start from, as that does not determine your destiny. What determines your destiny is trusting in God and working hard for what you want. There might be discouraging days but keep looking towards the dream goal.

You will not reach your goals if you stop dreaming. A winner is a dreamer who never gives up on what they are dreaming about.

My book focuses in depth on why giving up should not be an option. I know of people, including myself, who toiled hard for years without giving up and our dreams goals were accomplished through prayer, hard work and dedication.

Those of you who are thinking about giving up, please think twice. No situation is permanent. You may be down today, and up tomorrow. Believe in yourself. Tell yourself that you are going to make it. Ignore all the negative comments from those around you. Ignore all your own negative thoughts. Go for your dreams. Work hard to accomplish them. Always take care of yourself while working hard to reach your goals. Helping others along the way is an effective way of helping yourself. It will also motivate you to do better. Keep your eyes on the prize. When your eyes get tired, rest if you must, but focus on your dream goal.

My book will benefit those who are feeling depressed today. Those who are aching from one thing or another. Those who have been falsely accused. Those who are thinking about giving up. Those who had past failures. Those who feel broken. Those who feel lost. Those who are jobless and homeless. I want to remind you that God loves you.

## Book Summary

My book will also benefit those people who are having mental health challenges. Mental health is a vital and important topic today. We are living in serious and uncertain times and people are frustrated. People are losing faith and hope. Speaking about faith and hope, my book will tell you about these topics too.

I wrote about storms in my book. The perfect storm is when God allows us to go through the challenging times that will land us right into victory. Sometimes God allows us to go through the storm to build our faith then he brings us the calm for a brighter day. You may say there is no such thing as a perfect storm, but when victory comes through a storm, then you will understand. Sometimes storms happen for a reason.

# Acknowledgements

First, I must thank the good Lord for the amazing things he has done for me and my family.

Special thanks to my beautiful daughter Crystal Johnson for her continuing support and cooperation.

Thanks to one of my good friends Sahai Profitt who encouraged me to write a book of inspiration. She told me she liked the inspirational quotes I usually send to her. I took her advice and decided to write this book to encourage people in their journey of life.

Thanks also to the people on my gospel page The Message of the Cross who have been supporting me and my inspirational messages for years. Also, thanks to family and friends on my Facebook page and Instagram. It was an immense pleasure sharing those inspirational messages with you throughout the years. Thank you for your supporting comments.

Special thanks to the publishing team. I am so grateful and thankful for your continuing support and cooperation. Your communication skills and feedback are always clear and frequent. Questions are answered in a timely manner. Well done.

Thanks to everyone who continues to support me by buying my books and I look forward to your continuing support.

Special thanks to everyone at the company where I worked for your support and cooperation throughout the eight years. Thank you for supporting me in purchasing my previous books. I do appreciate it so much.

Thanks to my church family who has been incredibly supportive to me, especially everyone in our choir group. Thank you for giving me the privilege of singing in the choir. It was an amazing year with the group. The Christmas concert was amazing, and our choir did extremely well. The cultural concert was also amazing. Glory be to God.

Special thanks to all my family and friends. I pray that in 2024 God will grant us all a peaceful and happy year with good health and strength.

God is a good God.

www.ingramcontent.com/pod-product-compliance
Lightning Source LLC
Chambersburg PA
CBHW052149070526
44585CB00017B/2033